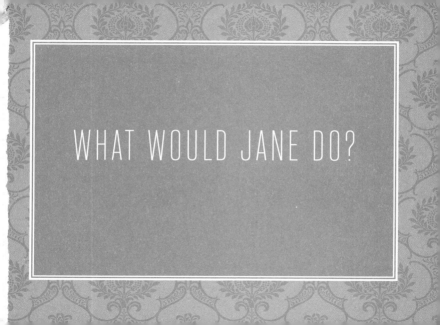

WHAT WOULD JANE DO?

WHAT WOULD JANE DO?

QUIPS AND WISDOM FROM JANE AUSTEN

Potter Style
New York

Published in the United States by Potter Style,
an imprint of the Crown Publishing Group,
a division of Random House LLC, a Penguin
Random House Company, New York.
www.crownpublishing.com
www.clarksonpotter.com

POTTER STYLE and colophon are registered
trademarks of Random House LLC.
Library of Congress Cataloging-in-Publication
Data is available upon request.
ISBN 978-0-8041-8562-2
Printed in China
Book and cover design by La Tricia Watford
10 9 8 7 6 5 4 3 2
First Edition

WHAT WOULD JANE DO?

I.

HOW TO BE HAPPIER
—
THAN YOU DESERVE

NEXT WEEK [I] SHALL BEGIN

MY OPERATIONS ON MY HAT,

ON WHICH YOU KNOW MY PRINCIPAL

HOPES OF HAPPINESS DEPEND.

—LETTERS

NOBODY MINDS

HAVING WHAT IS TOO GOOD

FOR THEM.

—MANSFIELD PARK (1814)

I WISH, AS WELL AS EVERYBODY ELSE,

TO BE PERFECTLY HAPPY;

BUT, LIKE EVERYBODY ELSE,

IT MUST BE IN MY OWN WAY.

—SENSE AND SENSIBILITY (1811)

IT IS WELL TO HAVE AS

MANY HOLDS UPON HAPPINESS

AS POSSIBLE.

—EMMA (1815)

I AM HAPPIER EVEN THAN JANE;

SHE ONLY SMILES,

I LAUGH.

—PRIDE AND PREJUDICE (1813)

HOW OFTEN IS

HAPPINESS DESTROYED

BY PREPARATION,

FOOLISH PREPARATION!

—LETTERS

WE ARE ALL APT TO EXPECT TOO MUCH;
BUT THEN, IF ONE SCHEME OF HAPPINESS FAILS,
HUMAN NATURE TURNS TO ANOTHER;
IF THE FIRST CALCULATION IS WRONG,
WE MAKE A SECOND BETTER:
WE FIND COMFORT SOMEWHERE.

—MANSFIELD PARK (1814)

PERFECT HAPPINESS,

EVEN IN MEMORY,

IS NOT COMMON.

—EMMA (1815)

HOW QUICK

COME THE REASONS FOR

APPROVING WHAT WE LIKE.

—PERSUASION (1817)

YOUR COUNTENANCE PERFECTLY INFORMS ME

THAT YOU WERE IN COMPANY

LAST NIGHT WITH THE PERSON WHO

INTERESTS YOU AT THIS PRESENT TIME,

MORE THAN ALL THE REST OF THE WORLD

PUT TOGETHER.

—PERSUASION (1817)

IN SEASONS OF CHEERFULNESS,

NO TEMPER COULD BE MORE CHEERFUL

THAN HERS, OR POSSESS, IN A GREATER DEGREE,

THAT SANGUINE EXPECTATION

OF HAPPINESS WHICH IS HAPPINESS ITSELF.

—SENSE AND SENSIBILITY (1811)

NOTHING EVER FATIGUES ME,

BUT DOING WHAT I DO NOT LIKE.

—MANSFIELD PARK (1814)

KNOW YOUR OWN HAPPINESS.

YOU WANT NOTHING BUT PATIENCE—

OR GIVE IT A MORE FASCINATING NAME,

CALL IT HOPE.

—SENSE AND SENSIBILITY (1811)

I MUST LEARN

TO BE CONTENT

WITH BEING

HAPPIER THAN I DESERVE.

—LETTERS

WHERE THE WATERS DO AGREE,

IT IS QUITE WONDERFUL

THE RELIEF THEY GIVE.

—EMMA (1815)

II.

GOOD IMPRESSIONS

—

FOR GREAT LADIES

EVERY NEIGHBORHOOD

SHOULD HAVE A GREAT LADY.

—SANDITON (1817)

ONE CAN NEVER

HAVE TOO LARGE A PARTY.

—PRIDE AND PREJUDICE (1813)

YOU ARE NEVER

SURE OF A GOOD IMPRESSION

BEING DURABLE.

—PERSUASION (1817)

SILLY THINGS

DO CEASE TO BE SILLY IF

THEY ARE DONE BY SENSIBLE PEOPLE

IN AN IMPUDENT WAY.

—EMMA (1815)

FOR WHAT DO WE LIVE,

BUT TO MAKE SPORT FOR

OUR NEIGHBORS AND

LAUGH AT THEM IN OUR TURN?

—PRIDE AND PREJUDICE (1813)

WE DO NOT

LOOK IN GREAT CITIES

FOR OUR BEST

MORALITY.

— MANSFIELD PARK (1814)

MY IDEA OF GOOD COMPANY . . .
IS THE COMPANY OF CLEVER,
WELL-INFORMED PEOPLE WHO
HAVE A GREAT DEAL OF CONVERSATION;
THAT IS WHAT I CALL GOOD COMPANY.

—PERSUASION (1817)

THOSE WHO DO NOT COMPLAIN

ARE NEVER PITIED.

—PRIDE AND PREJUDICE (1813)

THERE ARE SOME

PEOPLE WHO CANNOT BEAR

A PARTY OF PLEASURE.

—SENSE AND SENSIBILITY (1811)

ONE HALF OF THE WORLD

CANNOT UNDERSTAND

THE PLEASURES OF THE OTHER.

—EMMA (1815)

I SHOULD BUY A

LITTLE LAND AND BUILD ONE MYSELF,

WITHIN A SHORT DISTANCE OF LONDON. . . .

I ADVISE EVERYBODY

WHO IS GOING TO BUILD,

TO BUILD A COTTAGE.

—SENSE AND SENSIBILITY (1811)

EVERY MAN

IS SURROUNDED BY

A NEIGHBORHOOD OF

VOLUNTARY SPIES.

—NORTHANGER ABBEY (1817)

IT WAS A DELIGHTFUL VISIT;

—PERFECT,

IN BEING MUCH TOO SHORT.

—EMMA (1815)

IT IS PARTICULARLY INCUMBENT

ON THOSE WHO NEVER CHANGE

THEIR OPINION, TO BE SECURE OF

JUDGING PROPERLY

AT FIRST.

—PRIDE AND PREJUDICE (1813)

NOTHING AMUSES ME MORE
THAN THE EASY MANNER WITH WHICH
EVERYBODY SETTLES THE ABUNDANCE
OF THOSE WHO HAVE A GREAT DEAL
LESS THAN THEMSELVES.

—MANSFIELD PARK (1814)

SOMETIMES ONE IS GUIDED BY

WHAT THEY SAY OF THEMSELVES,

AND VERY FREQUENTLY BY WHAT

OTHER PEOPLE SAY OF THEM,

WITHOUT GIVING ONESELF TIME TO

DELIBERATE AND JUDGE.

—SENSE AND SENSIBILITY (1811)

FROM POLITICS,

IT WAS AN EASY STEP TO SILENCE.

— NORTHANGER ABBEY (1817)

I HAVE FREQUENTLY THOUGHT
THAT I MUST HAVE BEEN INTENDED BY
NATURE TO BE FOND OF LOW COMPANY,
I AM SO LITTLE AT MY EASE AMONG
STRANGERS OF GENTILITY!

—SENSE AND SENSIBILITY (1811)

I QUIT SUCH ODIOUS SUBJECTS

AS SOON AS I CAN,

IMPATIENT TO RESTORE EVERYBODY,

NOT GREATLY IN FAULT THEMSELVES,

TO TOLERABLE COMFORT.

—MANSFIELD PARK (1814)

BUT WHEN A YOUNG LADY IS TO BE A HEROINE,
THE PERVERSENESS OF FORTY
SURROUNDING FAMILIES CANNOT PREVENT HER.
SOMETHING MUST
AND WILL HAPPEN TO
THROW A HERO IN HER WAY.

— NORTHANGER ABBEY (1817)

WE ARE SENT INTO THIS WORLD
TO BE AS EXTENSIVELY USEFUL
AS POSSIBLE, AND WHERE SOME DEGREE OF
STRENGTH OF MIND IS GIVEN,
IT IS NOT A FEEBLE BODY WHICH
WILL EXCUSE US—OR INCLINE US TO
EXCUSE OURSELVES.

—SANDITON (1817)

III.

MISTRESS

—

OF MYSELF

NO ONE CAN THINK MORE
HIGHLY OF THE UNDERSTANDING OF WOMEN
THAN I DO . . . NATURE HAS GIVEN THEM SO
MUCH, THAT THEY NEVER FIND IT NECESSARY
TO USE MORE THAN HALF.

—NORTHANGER ABBEY (1817)

YOU WERE DISGUSTED

WITH THE WOMEN WHO WERE

ALWAYS SPEAKING AND LOOKING,

AND THINKING FOR YOUR APPROBATION ALONE.

I ROUSED, AND INTERESTED YOU,

BECAUSE I WAS SO UNLIKE THEM.

— PRIDE AND PREJUDICE (1813)

TO LOOK ALMOST PRETTY
IS AN ACQUISITION OF HIGHER DELIGHT
TO A GIRL WHO HAS BEEN LOOKING PLAIN
FOR THE FIRST FIFTEEN YEARS OF HER LIFE
THAN A BEAUTY FROM HER CRADLE
CAN EVER RECEIVE.

—NORTHANGER ABBEY (1817)

YOU MUST TRY NOT TO MIND

GROWING UP INTO A PRETTY

WOMAN.

—MANSFIELD PARK (1814)

AS FOR ADMIRATION,

IT WAS ALWAYS VERY WELCOME WHEN IT CAME,

BUT SHE DID NOT DEPEND ON IT.

—NORTHANGER ABBEY (1817)

HER OWN
THOUGHTS AND REFLECTIONS
WERE HABITUALLY
HER BEST COMPANIONS.

—MANSFIELD PARK (1814)

I ALWAYS

DESERVE THE BEST TREATMENT

BECAUSE I NEVER PUT UP WITH ANY OTHER.

—EMMA (1815)

LAUGH AS MUCH AS YOU CHOOSE,

BUT YOU WILL NOT

LAUGH ME OUT OF MY OPINION.

—PRIDE AND PREJUDICE (1813)

THERE ARE PEOPLE WHO

THE MORE YOU DO FOR THEM,

THE LESS THEY WILL DO

FOR THEMSELVES.

—EMMA (1815)

IT ISN'T

WHAT WE SAY OR THINK

THAT DEFINES US,

BUT WHAT WE DO.

—SENSE AND SENSIBILITY (1811)

IF I COULD NOT BE PERSUADED
INTO DOING WHAT I THOUGHT WRONG,
I WILL NEVER BE TRICKED INTO IT.

— NORTHANGER ABBEY (1817)

I HAVE BEEN A

SELFISH BEING ALL MY LIFE,

IN PRACTICE,

THOUGH NOT IN PRINCIPLE.

—PRIDE AND PREJUDICE (1813)

WE ALL HAVE

OUR BEST GUIDES WITHIN US,

IF ONLY WE WOULD LISTEN.

—MANSFIELD PARK (1814)

I SPEAK

WHAT APPEARS TO ME THE GENERAL OPINION; AND

WHERE AN OPINION IS GENERAL,

IT IS USUALLY CORRECT.

— MANSFIELD PARK (1814)

THERE IS HARDLY

ANY PERSONAL DEFECT

WHICH AN AGREEABLE MANNER

MIGHT NOT

GRADUALLY RECONCILE ONE TO.

—NORTHANGER ABBEY (1817)

IF I COULD PERSUADE MYSELF

THAT MY MANNERS

WERE PERFECTLY

EASY AND GRACEFUL,

I SHOULD NOT BE SHY.

— SENSE AND SENSIBILITY (1811)

THOSE

WHO HAVE NOT MORE

MUST BE SATISFIED

WITH WHAT THEY HAVE.

—MANSFIELD PARK (1814)

I AM ONLY RESOLVED

TO ACT IN THAT MANNER,

WHICH WILL, IN MY OWN OPINION,

CONSTITUTE MY HAPPINESS,

WITHOUT REFERENCE TO YOU.

— PRIDE AND PREJUDICE (1813)

LET

YOUR CONDUCT

BE THE ONLY

HARANGUE.

—MANSFIELD PARK (1814)

MY BEING CHARMING . . .
IS NOT QUITE ENOUGH
TO INDUCE ME TO MARRY;
I MUST FIND OTHER PEOPLE CHARMING—
ONE OTHER PERSON AT LEAST.

—EMMA (1815)

PLEASED WITH THE PREFERENCE OF ONE,

AND OFFENDED BY THE NEGLECT OF THE OTHER,

ON THE VERY BEGINNING OF OUR ACQUAINTANCE,

I HAVE COURTED PREPOSSESSION

AND IGNORANCE, AND DRIVEN REASON AWAY. . . .

TILL THIS MOMENT I NEVER KNEW MYSELF.

—PRIDE AND PREJUDICE (1813)

I WILL BE CALM.

I WILL BE MISTRESS OF MYSELF.

—SENSE AND SENSIBILITY (1811)

RUN MAD

AS OFTEN AS YOU CHOOSE,

BUT DO NOT FAINT.

— MANSFIELD PARK (1814)

IV.

CHECK YOURSELF,

—— DEAR

IT IS VERY OFTEN
NOTHING BUT OUR OWN VANITY
THAT DECEIVES US.
WOMEN FANCY ADMIRATION
MEANS MORE THAN IT DOES.

—PRIDE AND PREJUDICE (1813)

A PERSON MAY BE PROUD
WITHOUT BEING VAIN.
PRIDE RELATES MORE TO OUR
OPINION OF OURSELVES; VANITY,
TO WHAT WE WOULD HAVE
OTHERS THINK OF US.

—PRIDE AND PREJUDICE (1813)

I MAKE NO APOLOGIES
FOR MY HEROINE'S VANITY.
IF THERE ARE YOUNG LADIES
IN THE WORLD AT HER TIME OF LIFE
MORE DULL OF FANCY AND
MORE CARELESS OF PLEASING, I KNOW THEM NOT.

— SANDITON (1817)

SUCH SQUEAMISH YOUTHS

AS CANNOT BEAR TO BE CONNECTED

WITH A LITTLE ABSURDITY

ARE NOT WORTH A REGRET.

—PRIDE AND PREJUDICE (1813)

WHERE YOUTH AND DIFFIDENCE ARE UNITED,
IT REQUIRES UNCOMMON STEADINESS
OF REASON TO RESIST THE ATTRACTION OF
BEING CALLED THE MOST
CHARMING GIRL IN THE WORLD.

—NORTHANGER ABBEY (1817)

BUT THAT IS

ONE GREAT DIFFERENCE BETWEEN

US. COMPLIMENTS ALWAYS

TAKE YOU BY SURPRISE,

AND ME NEVER.

— PRIDE AND PREJUDICE (1813)

ONE IS APT, I BELIEVE,

TO CONNECT ASSURANCE OF MANNER

WITH COQUETRY, AND TO EXPECT THAT

AN IMPUDENT ADDRESS

WILL NATURALLY ATTEND AN IMPUDENT MIND.

—LADY SUSAN (1794)

VANITY WORKING

ON A WEAK HEAD PRODUCES

EVERY SORT OF MISCHIEF.

—EMMA (1815)

PICTURES OF PERFECTION,

AS YOU KNOW,

MAKE ME SICK AND WICKED.

—LETTERS

SELDOM, VERY SELDOM,

DOES COMPLETE TRUTH BELONG TO

ANY HUMAN DISCLOSURE;

SELDOM CAN IT HAPPEN THAT SOMETHING IS

NOT A LITTLE DISGUISED,

OR A LITTLE MISTAKEN.

—EMMA (1815)

SENSE WILL ALWAYS

HAVE ATTRACTIONS FOR ME.

—SENSE AND SENSIBILITY (1811)

I CANNOT SPEAK WELL ENOUGH

TO BE UNINTELLIGIBLE.

—NORTHANGER ABBEY (1817)

BETTER BE

WITHOUT SENSE THAN MISAPPLY IT

AS YOU DO.

—EMMA (1815)

WISDOM

IS BETTER THAN WIT,

AND IN THE LONG RUN WILL CERTAINLY

HAVE THE LAUGH ON HER SIDE.

—LETTERS

[SHE] IS ONE OF THOSE YOUNG LADIES WHO
SEEK TO RECOMMEND THEMSELVES
TO THE OTHER SEX BY
UNDERVALUING THEIR OWN. . . .
BUT, IN MY OPINION,
IT IS A PALTRY DEVICE, A VERY MEAN ART.

—PRIDE AND PREJUDICE (1813)

NEXT TO BEING MARRIED,
A GIRL LIKES TO BE CROSSED IN LOVE
A LITTLE NOW AND THEN.
IT IS SOMETHING TO THINK OF,
AND GIVES HER A SORT OF DISTINCTION
AMONG HER COMPANIONS.

—PRIDE AND PREJUDICE (1813)

ALL THE PRIVILEGE

I CLAIM FOR MY OWN SEX . . .

IS THAT OF LOVING LONGEST,

WHEN EXISTENCE OR WHEN HOPE IS GONE.

—PERSUASION (1817)

HER CHARACTER

DEPENDS UPON THOSE SHE IS WITH;

BUT IN GOOD HANDS SHE WILL

TURN OUT A VALUABLE WOMAN.

—EMMA (1815)

IN NINE CASES OUT OF TEN,

A WOMAN HAD BETTER SHOW

MORE AFFECTION THAN SHE FEELS.

—PRIDE AND PREJUDICE (1813)

SHE DENIED NONE

OF IT ALOUD,

AND AGREED TO NONE OF IT

IN PRIVATE.

—EMMA (1815)

I HATE TO HEAR YOU TALKING . . .

AS IF WOMEN WERE ALL FINE LADIES

INSTEAD OF RATIONAL CREATURES.

WE NONE OF US EXPECT TO

BE IN SMOOTH WATER ALL OUR DAYS.

— PERSUASION (1817)

A LADY'S IMAGINATION IS VERY RAPID;

IT JUMPS FROM ADMIRATION

TO LOVE, FROM LOVE TO MATRIMONY

IN A MOMENT.

—PRIDE AND PREJUDICE (1813)

A LADY,

WITHOUT A FAMILY,

WAS THE VERY BEST PRESERVER OF

FURNITURE IN THE WORLD.

—PERSUASION (1817)

IT SOMETIMES HAPPENS THAT

A WOMAN IS HANDSOMER

AT TWENTY-NINE

THAN SHE WAS TEN YEARS BEFORE.

—PERSUASION (1817)

WOMAN IS FINE FOR

HER OWN SATISFACTION ALONE.

NO MAN WILL ADMIRE HER

THE MORE,

NO WOMAN WILL LIKE HER THE BETTER FOR IT.

— NORTHANGER ABBEY (1817)

GIVE A GIRL AN EDUCATION AND
INTRODUCE HER PROPERLY INTO THE WORLD,
AND TEN TO ONE BUT SHE HAS
THE MEANS OF SETTLING WELL,
WITHOUT FURTHER EXPENSE TO ANYBODY.

—MANSFIELD PARK (1814)

SHE WAS SENSIBLE AND CLEVER,

BUT EAGER IN EVERYTHING;

HER SORROWS, HER JOYS,

COULD HAVE NO MODERATION.

—SENSE AND SENSIBILITY (1811)

SHE WAS DETERMINED,

AS SHE FELT IT TO BE HER DUTY,

TO TRY TO OVERCOME

ALL THAT WAS EXCESSIVE.

—MANSFIELD PARK (1814)

SHE FELT THAT SHE COULD SO MUCH MORE

DEPEND UPON THE SINCERITY OF

THOSE WHO SOMETIMES LOOKED OR SAID

A CARELESS OR A HASTY THING,

THAN OF THOSE WHOSE PRESENCE OF MIND

NEVER VARIED, WHOSE TONGUE NEVER SLIPPED.

— PERSUASION (1817)

DO NOT CONSIDER ME NOW AS

AN ELEGANT FEMALE

INTENDING TO PLAGUE YOU, BUT

AS A RATIONAL CREATURE

SPEAKING THE TRUTH FROM HER HEART.

—PRIDE AND PREJUDICE (1813)

THE ENTHUSIASM OF

A WOMAN'S LOVE

IS EVEN BEYOND THE BIOGRAPHER'S.

—MANSFIELD PARK (1814)

V.

GET TO KNOW YOUR

GENTLEMAN

WHAT STRANGE

CREATURES

BROTHERS ARE!

—MANSFIELD PARK (1814)

THE LADIES HERE PROBABLY
EXCHANGED LOOKS WHICH MEANT,
"MEN NEVER KNOW WHEN THINGS
ARE DIRTY OR NOT;" AND THE GENTLEMEN
PERHAPS THOUGHT EACH TO HIMSELF,
"WOMEN WILL HAVE THEIR LITTLE
NONSENSE AND NEEDLESS CARES."

—EMMA (1815)

A MAN DOES NOT

RECOVER FROM SUCH DEVOTION

OF THE HEART

TO SUCH A WOMAN!

HE OUGHT NOT; HE DOES NOT.

—PERSUASION (1817)

GENERAL

BENEVOLENCE,

BUT NOT GENERAL FRIENDSHIP,

MADE A MAN

WHAT HE OUGHT TO BE.

—EMMA (1815)

IF THERE IS ANY THING

DISAGREEABLE GOING ON,

MEN ARE ALWAYS SURE TO GET OUT OF IT.

— PERSUASION (1817)

WITH MEN HE CAN
BE RATIONAL AND UNAFFECTED,
BUT WHEN HE HAS LADIES TO PLEASE,
EVERY FEATURE WORKS.

—EMMA (1815)

[HE] IS JUST THE TYPE OF MAN . . .
WHOM EVERYBODY SPEAKS WELL OF,
AND NOBODY CARES ABOUT;
WHOM ALL ARE DELIGHTED TO SEE,
AND NOBODY REMEMBERS TO TALK TO.

—SENSE AND SENSIBILITY (1811)

MEN OF SENSE,

WHATEVER YOU MAY CHOOSE TO SAY,

DO NOT WANT SILLY WIVES.

—EMMA (1815)

HE THOROUGHLY KNOWS

HIS OWN MIND,

AND ACTS UP TO HIS RESOLUTIONS:

AN INESTIMABLE QUALITY.

—MANSFIELD PARK (1814)

IT WOULD BE MORTIFYING
TO THE FEELINGS OF MANY LADIES,
COULD THEY BE MADE
TO UNDERSTAND HOW LITTLE
THE HEART OF MAN IS AFFECTED BY
WHAT IS COSTLY OR
NEW IN THEIR ATTIRE.

—NORTHANGER ABBEY (1817)

THERE CERTAINLY

ARE NOT SO MANY MEN OF

LARGE FORTUNE IN THE WORLD,

AS THERE ARE PRETTY WOMEN

TO DESERVE THEM.

—MANSFIELD PARK (1814)

ONE MAN'S WAYS

MAY BE AS GOOD AS ANOTHER'S,

BUT WE ALL LIKE OUR OWN BEST.

—PERSUASION (1817)

WE ALL KNOW HIM TO BE A PROUD,

UNPLEASANT SORT OF A MAN;

BUT THIS WOULD BE NOTHING

IF YOU REALLY LIKED HIM.

—PRIDE AND PREJUDICE (1813)

I COULD EASILY

FORGIVE HIS PRIDE,

IF HE HAD NOT MORTIFIED MINE.

— SENSE AND SENSIBILITY (1811)

YOU ARE MISTAKEN, MR. DARCY,
IF YOU SUPPOSE THAT THE MODE OF YOUR
DECLARATION AFFECTED ME IN ANY OTHER WAY,
THAN AS IT SPARED ME THE CONCERN WHICH
I MIGHT HAVE FELT IN REFUSING YOU,
HAD YOU BEHAVED IN A MORE
GENTLEMAN-LIKE MANNER.

—PRIDE AND PREJUDICE (1813)

DARE NOT SAY

THAT MAN FORGETS SOONER

THAN WOMAN, THAT

HIS LOVE HAS AN EARLIER DEATH.

— PERSUASION (1817)

FROM THE FIRST MOMENT,

I MAY ALMOST SAY . . .

I HAD NOT KNOWN YOU A MONTH BEFORE I FELT

THAT YOU WERE THE LAST MAN

IN THE WORLD WHOM I COULD EVER BE

PREVAILED ON TO MARRY.

—PRIDE AND PREJUDICE (1813)

THAT WOULD BE THE
GREATEST MISFORTUNE OF ALL!—
TO FIND A MAN AGREEABLE
WHOM ONE IS DETERMINED TO HATE!—
DO NOT WISH ME SUCH AN EVIL.

—PRIDE AND PREJUDICE (1813)

SHE DID NOT THINK HE

DESERVED THE COMPLIMENT OF

RATIONAL OPPOSITION.

—SENSE AND SENSIBILITY (1811)

HIS COLD POLITENESS,

HIS CEREMONIOUS GRACE,

WERE WORSE THAN ANYTHING.

—PERSUASION (1817)

I COULD NOT BE HAPPY WITH

A MAN WHOSE TASTE

DID NOT IN EVERY POINT

COINCIDE WITH MY OWN.

—SENSE AND SENSIBILITY (1811)

STUPID MEN

ARE THE ONLY ONES

WORTH KNOWING,

AFTER ALL.

—PRIDE AND PREJUDICE (1813)

NOW THEY WERE AS STRANGERS;

NAY WORSE THAN STRANGERS,

FOR THEY COULD NEVER BECOME ACQUAINTED.

—PERSUASION (1817)

VI.

IF YOU

—

REALLY LIKE HIM

I SUPPOSE THERE MAY BE

A HUNDRED DIFFERENT WAYS

OF BEING IN LOVE.

—EMMA (1815)

THE VERY FIRST

MOMENT I BEHELD HIM,

MY HEART WAS IRREVOCABLY GONE.

—LOVE AND FRIENDSHIP (1790)

THE MORE I KNOW OF THE WORLD,

THE MORE I AM CONVINCED

THAT I SHALL NEVER SEE A MAN WHOM

I CAN REALLY LOVE.

I REQUIRE SO MUCH!

—SENSE AND SENSIBILITY (1811)

IN VAIN I HAVE STRUGGLED.

IT WILL NOT DO.

MY FEELINGS WILL NOT BE REPRESSED.

YOU MUST ALLOW ME TO TELL YOU

HOW ARDENTLY I ADMIRE AND LOVE YOU.

—PRIDE AND PREJUDICE (1813)

THERE IS NOTHING I WOULD NOT DO FOR
THOSE WHO ARE REALLY MY FRIENDS.
I HAVE NO NOTION OF LOVING PEOPLE BY HALVES,
IT IS NOT MY NATURE.

—NORTHANGER ABBEY (1817)

HE IS A GENTLEMAN, AND

I AM A GENTLEMAN'S DAUGHTER.

SO FAR WE ARE EQUAL.

—PRIDE AND PREJUDICE (1813)

TO HER OWN HEART IT
WAS A DELIGHTFUL AFFAIR,
TO HER IMAGINATION IT WAS
EVEN A RIDICULOUS ONE,
BUT TO HER REASON, HER JUDGMENT,
IT WAS COMPLETELY A PUZZLE.

—SENSE AND SENSIBILITY (1811)

THERE ARE SUCH BEINGS IN THE WORLD . . .

AS THE CREATURE

YOU AND I SHOULD THINK PERFECTION . . .

BUT SUCH A PERSON

MAY NOT COME IN YOUR WAY.

—LETTERS

IF I COULD BUT KNOW

HIS HEART,

EVERYTHING WOULD BECOME EASY.

—SENSE AND SENSIBILITY (1811)

TO FLATTER AND FOLLOW OTHERS,

WITHOUT BEING FLATTERED

AND FOLLOWED IN TURN, IS BUT

A STATE OF HALF ENJOYMENT.

—PERSUASION (1817)

NO MAN IS OFFENDED BY

ANOTHER MAN'S ADMIRATION

OF THE WOMAN HE LOVES;

IT IS THE WOMAN ONLY WHO

CAN MAKE IT A TORMENT.

—NORTHANGER ABBEY (1817)

**HOW LITTLE OF
PERMANENT HAPPINESS COULD
BELONG TO A COUPLE WHO
WERE ONLY BROUGHT TOGETHER
BECAUSE THEIR PASSIONS WERE
STRONGER THAN THEIR VIRTUE.**

—PRIDE AND PREJUDICE (1813)

THERE COULD HAVE BEEN

NO TWO HEARTS SO OPEN,

NO TASTES SO SIMILAR,

NO FEELINGS SO IN UNISON.

—PERSUASION (1817)

SHE WAS CONVINCED THAT

SHE COULD HAVE BEEN HAPPY

WITH HIM,

WHEN IT WAS NO LONGER

LIKELY THEY SHOULD MEET.

—PRIDE AND PREJUDICE (1813)

YOU PIERCE MY SOUL.

I AM HALF AGONY,

HALF HOPE . . . I HAVE LOVED NONE BUT YOU.

—PERSUASION (1817)

WERE I TO FALL IN LOVE, INDEED,

IT WOULD BE A DIFFERENT THING;

BUT I HAVE NEVER BEEN IN LOVE;

IT IS NOT MY WAY, OR MY NATURE;

AND I DO NOT THINK I EVER SHALL.

—EMMA (1815)

IT IS MY

UNHAPPY FATE

SELDOM TO TREAT PEOPLE AS WELL

AS THEY DESERVE.

—LETTERS

THIS SENSATION OF LISTLESSNESS, WEARINESS,
STUPIDITY, THIS DISINCLINATION TO SIT DOWN
AND EMPLOY MYSELF, THIS FEELING OF EVERY-
THING'S BEING DULL AND INSIPID ABOUT THE
HOUSE! I MUST BE IN LOVE; I SHOULD BE THE ODD-
EST CREATURE IN THE WORLD IF I WERE NOT.

—EMMA (1815)

HAD I NOT BEEN BOUND TO SILENCE

I COULD HAVE PROVIDED PROOF

ENOUGH OF A

BROKEN HEART, EVEN FOR YOU.

—SENSE AND SENSIBILITY (1811)

THEY PARTED AT LAST

WITH MUTUAL CIVILITY,

AND POSSIBLY A MUTUAL DESIRE OF

NEVER MEETING AGAIN.

—PRIDE AND PREJUDICE (1813)

IT WOULD BE DIFFICULT TO SAY WHICH HAD

SEEN HIGHEST PERFECTION

IN THE OTHER,

OR WHICH HAD BEEN THE HAPPIEST:

SHE, IN RECEIVING HIS

DECLARATIONS AND PROPOSALS,

OR HE IN HAVING THEM ACCEPTED.

—PERSUASION (1817)

I LAY IT DOWN AS A GENERAL RULE . . .

THAT IF A WOMAN DOUBTS

AS TO WHETHER SHE SHOULD

ACCEPT A MAN OR NOT,

SHE CERTAINLY OUGHT TO REFUSE HIM.

—EMMA (1815)

WHEN I FALL IN LOVE,

IT WILL BE FOREVER.

—SENSE AND SENSIBILITY (1811)

TO LOVE

IS TO BURN,

TO BE ON FIRE.

—SENSE AND SENSIBILITY (1811)

IF I LOVED YOU LESS,

I MIGHT BE ABLE TO TALK ABOUT IT MORE.

—EMMA (1815)

SOMETIMES THE LAST PERSON

ON EARTH YOU WANT TO BE WITH

IS THE ONE PERSON

YOU CAN'T BE WITHOUT.

—PRIDE AND PREJUDICE (1813)

HAPPINESS

IN MARRIAGE

IS ENTIRELY

A MATTER OF CHANCE.

—PRIDE AND PREJUDICE (1813)

MARRIAGE

IS INDEED

A MANEUVERING BUSINESS.

—MANSFIELD PARK (1814)

YOU MISTAKE ME, MY DEAR.

I HAVE THE UTMOST RESPECT

FOR YOUR NERVES. THEY'VE BEEN

MY CONSTANT COMPANION

THESE TWENTY YEARS.

—PRIDE AND PREJUDICE (1813)

HUSBANDS AND WIVES

GENERALLY UNDERSTAND

WHEN OPPOSITION WILL BE VAIN.

—PERSUASION (1817)

I PAY VERY LITTLE REGARD . . . TO
WHAT ANY YOUNG PERSON SAYS
ON THE SUBJECT OF MARRIAGE.
IF THEY PROFESS A DISINCLINATION
FOR IT, I ONLY SET IT DOWN THAT THEY
HAVE NOT YET SEEN THE RIGHT PERSON.

—MANSFIELD PARK (1814)

VII.

INTIMATE

———

ACQUAINTANCES

SEVEN YEARS WOULD BE INSUFFICIENT
TO MAKE SOME PEOPLE ACQUAINTED
WITH EACH OTHER AND SEVEN DAYS ARE
MORE THAN ENOUGH FOR OTHERS.

—SENSE AND SENSIBILITY (1811)

MY GOOD QUALITIES ARE UNDER YOUR
PROTECTION, AND YOU ARE TO EXAGGERATE THEM
AS MUCH AS POSSIBLE; AND, IN RETURN, IT
BELONGS TO ME TO FIND OCCASION FOR TEASING
AND QUARRELING WITH YOU AS OFTEN AS MAY BE.

—PRIDE AND PREJUDICE (1813)

I DEARLY LOVE A LAUGH . . .

I HOPE I NEVER RIDICULE

WHAT IS WISE OR GOOD.

—PRIDE AND PREJUDICE (1813)

ONE LOVES

TO LOOK AT AN OLD FRIEND

AT A PLACE

WHERE ONE HAS BEEN HAPPY.

—SANDITON (1817)

ONE HAD RATHER,

ON SUCH OCCASIONS,

DO TOO MUCH

THAN TOO LITTLE.

—SENSE AND SENSIBILITY (1811)

I OFTEN THINK, . . . THAT THERE IS

NOTHING SO BAD AS PARTING

WITH ONE'S FRIENDS.

ONE SEEMS SO FORLORN

WITHOUT THEM.

— PRIDE AND PREJUDICE (1813)

**THERE IS A QUICKNESS OF PERCEPTION
IN SOME, A NICETY IN THE DISCERNMENT
OF CHARACTER, A NATURAL PENETRATION,
IN SHORT, WHICH NO EXPERIENCE IN
OTHERS CAN EQUAL.**

—PERSUASION (1817)

VIII.

SENSIBLE QUIPS

—

FOR EVERY OCCASION

I WILL NOT SAY THAT YOUR
MULBERRY-TREES ARE DEAD,
BUT I AM AFRAID
THEY ARE NOT ALIVE.

—LETTERS

MARY WISHED TO SAY SOMETHING

VERY SENSIBLE,

BUT KNEW NOT HOW.

—PRIDE AND PREJUDICE (1813)

I WISH

WITH ALL MY SOUL

HIS WIFE MAY PLAGUE

HIS HEART OUT.

—SENSE AND SENSIBILITY (1811)

AFTER ABUSING YOU

SO ABOMINABLY TO YOUR FACE,

I COULD HAVE NO

SCRUPLE IN ABUSING YOU

TO ALL YOUR RELATIONS.

—PRIDE AND PREJUDICE (1813)

WHERE THERE IS

A DISPOSITION TO DISLIKE,

A MOTIVE WILL NEVER BE WANTING.

—LADY SUSAN (1794)

IF WE HAVE NOT HEARTS,

WE HAVE EYES;

AND THEY GIVE US

TORMENT ENOUGH.

—NORTHANGER ABBEY (1817)

I AM SORRY TO TELL YOU THAT I AM
GETTING VERY EXTRAVAGANT AND SPENDING
ALL MY MONEY: AND WHAT IS WORSE FOR YOU,
I HAVE BEEN SPENDING YOURS TOO.

—LETTERS

I ASSURE YOU.

I HAVE NO NOTION OF

TREATING MEN WITH SUCH RESPECT.

THAT IS THE WAY TO SPOIL THEM.

—NORTHANGER ABBEY (1817)

YOU EXPECT ME TO

ACCOUNT FOR OPINIONS

WHICH YOU CHOOSE TO CALL MINE,

BUT WHICH I HAVE NEVER

ACKNOWLEDGED.

—PRIDE AND PREJUDICE (1813)

I AM NOT FOND OF THE IDEA

OF MY SHRUBBERIES

BEING ALWAYS APPROACHABLE.

—PERSUASION (1817)

I DO NOT COUGH FOR MY OWN

AMUSEMENT.

—PRIDE AND PREJUDICE (1813)

I DO NOT WANT

PEOPLE TO BE VERY AGREEABLE,

AS IT SAVES ME THE TROUBLE OF

LIKING THEM A GREAT DEAL.

—LETTERS

MY GOOD OPINION

ONCE LOST IS LOST FOREVER.

— PRIDE AND PREJUDICE (1813)

IT IS NOT EVERYONE, . . . WHO HAS

YOUR PASSION FOR DEAD LEAVES.

—SENSE AND SENSIBILITY (1811)

IT IS HAPPY FOR YOU THAT YOU POSSESS
THE TALENT OF FLATTERING WITH DELICACY.
MAY I ASK WHETHER THESE PLEASING
ATTENTIONS PROCEED FROM THE
IMPULSE OF THE MOMENT, OR ARE THEY
THE RESULT OF PREVIOUS STUDY?

— PRIDE AND PREJUDICE (1813)

YOUR SILENCE

ON THE SUBJECT OF OUR BALL

MAKES ME SUPPOSE YOUR CURIOSITY

TOO GREAT FOR WORDS.

—LETTERS

I HAVE NOT

THE PLEASURE

OF UNDERSTANDING YOU.

—PRIDE AND PREJUDICE (1813)

IX.

I'D RATHER BE

————

WITH A BOOK

WHICH OF ALL MY

IMPORTANT NOTHINGS

SHALL I TELL YOU

FIRST?

—LETTERS

HOW MUCH SOONER ONE TIRES OF ANY THING

THAN OF A BOOK!—

WHEN I HAVE A HOUSE OF MY OWN,

I SHALL BE MISERABLE

IF I HAVE NOT AN EXCELLENT LIBRARY.

—PRIDE AND PREJUDICE (1813)

THE PERSON,

BE IT GENTLEMAN OR LADY,

WHO HAS NOT PLEASURE IN A GOOD NOVEL

MUST BE INTOLERABLY STUPID.

—NORTHANGER ABBEY (1817)

EXPECT A MOST AGREEABLE LETTER,

FOR NOT BEING OVERBURDENED

WITH SUBJECT (HAVING NOTHING AT ALL TO SAY),

I SHALL HAVE NO CHECK TO MY

GENIUS FROM BEGINNING TO END.

— LETTERS

WITH A BOOK

HE WAS REGARDLESS OF TIME.

— PRIDE AND PREJUDICE (1813)

LET OTHER PENS DWELL

ON GUILT AND MISERY.

—MANSFIELD PARK (1814)

INDULGE YOUR

IMAGINATION

IN EVERY

POSSIBLE FLIGHT.

—LETTERS

I ABHOR

EVERY

COMMON-PLACE PHRASE

BY WHICH WIT IS INTENDED.

—SENSE AND SENSIBILITY (1811)

OH! WRITE, WRITE.

FINISH IT AT ONCE.

LET THERE BE AN

END OF THIS SUSPENSE.

FIX, COMMIT, CONDEMN YOURSELF.

—MANSFIELD PARK (1814)

AN

ARTIST CANNOT

DO ANYTHING

SLOVENLY.

—LETTERS

AND TO ALL THIS SHE MUST YET ADD

SOMETHING MORE SUBSTANTIAL,

IN THE IMPROVEMENT OF HER MIND

BY EXTENSIVE READING.

—PRIDE AND PREJUDICE (1813)

OH! I AM DELIGHTED

WITH THE BOOK!

I SHOULD LIKE TO SPEND

MY WHOLE LIFE IN READING IT.

—NORTHANGER ABBEY (1817)

NOT KEEP A JOURNAL! . . .

HOW ARE YOUR VARIOUS DRESSES TO BE

REMEMBERED, AND THE PARTICULAR STATE OF

YOUR COMPLEXION, AND CURL OF YOUR HAIR TO

BE DESCRIBED IN ALL THEIR DIVERSITIES?

—NORTHANGER ABBEY (1817)

A PERSON WHO CAN

WRITE A LONG LETTER WITH EASE,

CANNOT WRITE ILL.

—PRIDE AND PREJUDICE (1813)

A FONDNESS FOR

READING . . .

PROPERLY DIRECTED,

MUST BE AN EDUCATION

IN ITSELF.

—MANSFIELD PARK (1814)

I AM NOT AT ALL

IN A HUMOUR FOR WRITING;

I MUST WRITE ON TILL I AM.

—LETTERS

IF THE HEROINE OF ONE NOVEL

BE NOT PATRONIZED BY THE

HEROINE OF ANOTHER,

FROM WHOM CAN SHE EXPECT

PROTECTION AND REGARD?

—NORTHANGER ABBEY (1817)

I THINK I MAY BOAST MYSELF TO BE,

WITH ALL POSSIBLE VANITY,

THE MOST UNLEARNED AND UNINFORMED

FEMALE WHO EVER DARED

TO BE AN

AUTHORESS.

—LETTERS

IT IS VERY WORTHWHILE

TO BE TORMENTED

FOR TWO OR THREE YEARS

OF ONE'S LIFE,

FOR THE SAKE OF BEING ABLE TO

READ ALL THE REST OF IT.

—NORTHANGER ABBEY (1817)

FOR MY OWN PART,

IF A BOOK IS WELL WRITTEN,

I ALWAYS FIND IT TOO SHORT.

—NORTHANGER ABBEY (1817)

THE NOVELS WHICH I APPROVE ARE SUCH AS
DISPLAY HUMAN NATURE WITH GRANDEUR;
SUCH AS SHOW HER IN THE SUBLIMITIES OF
INTENSE FEELING.

—SANDITON (1817)

I BEGIN ALREADY TO WEIGH MY WORDS &
SENTENCES MORE THAN I DID, & AM LOOKING
ABOUT FOR A SENTIMENT, AN ILLUSTRATION,
OR A METAPHOR IN EVERY CORNER OF THE ROOM.
COULD MY IDEAS FLOW AS FAST AS THE RAIN IN
THE STORECLOSET IT WOULD BE CHARMING.

—LETTERS

BY READING ONLY SIX HOURS A DAY,

I SHALL GAIN

IN THE COURSE OF A TWELVEMONTH

A GREAT DEAL OF INSTRUCTION

WHICH I NOW FEEL MYSELF TO WANT.

—SENSE AND SENSIBILITY (1811)

X.

LOOKING BACK ON

IMPORTANT NOTHINGS

LIFE SEEMS BUT

A QUICK SUCCESSION OF BUSY NOTHINGS.

—MANSFIELD PARK (1814)

THERE ARE AS

MANY FORMS OF LOVE

AS THERE ARE

MOMENTS IN TIME.

—LETTERS

IF THINGS ARE GOING

UNTOWARDLY ONE MONTH,

THEY ARE SURE TO MEND THE NEXT.

—EMMA (1815)

THINK ONLY

OF THE PAST

AS ITS REMEMBRANCE

GIVES YOU PLEASURE.

—PRIDE AND PREJUDICE (1813)

TIME WILL GENERALLY LESSEN THE

INTEREST OF EVERY ATTACHMENT

NOT WITHIN THE DAILY CIRCLE.

—EMMA (1815)

SHE CONSIDERED THAT THERE WERE
MISFORTUNES OF A MUCH GREATER MAGNITUDE
THAN THE LOSS OF A BALL AND THAT THE TIME
MIGHT COME WHEN SHE WOULD HERSELF LOOK
BACK WITH WONDER AND PERHAPS ENVY ON HER
HAVING KNOWN NO GREATER VEXATION.

— NORTHANGER ABBEY (1817)

AN INTERVAL OF MEDITATION,

SERIOUS AND GRATEFUL,

WAS THE BEST CORRECTIVE

OF EVERYTHING DANGEROUS.

—PERSUASION (1817)

THIS IS AN EVENING

OF WONDERS, INDEED!

—PRIDE AND PREJUDICE (1813)

EVERY MOMENT HAS

ITS PLEASURES AND ITS HOPE.

—MANSFIELD PARK (1814)

ONE DOES NOT LOVE A PLACE THE LESS FOR

HAVING SUFFERED IN IT,

UNLESS IT HAS BEEN ALL SUFFERING,

NOTHING BUT SUFFERING.

—PRIDE AND PREJUDICE (1813)

IF ANY ONE FACULTY OF OUR NATURE
MAY BE CALLED MORE WONDERFUL THAN
THE REST, I DO THINK IT IS MEMORY. THERE SEEMS
SOMETHING MORE SPEAKINGLY
INCOMPREHENSIBLE IN THE POWERS, THE
FAILURES, THE INEQUALITIES OF MEMORY,
THAN IN ANY OTHER OF OUR INTELLIGENCES.

—MANSFIELD PARK (1814)

THEY WALKED ON, WITHOUT

KNOWING IN WHAT DIRECTION.

THERE WAS TOO MUCH TO BE THOUGHT,

AND FELT, AND SAID,

FOR ATTENTION TO ANY OTHER OBJECTS.

—PRIDE AND PREJUDICE (1813)

YOU HAVE ANOTHER

LONG WALK BEFORE YOU.

—EMMA (1815)

REAL SOLEMN HISTORY,

I CANNOT BE INTERESTED IN . . .

THE MEN ALL SO GOOD FOR NOTHING,

AND HARDLY ANY WOMEN AT ALL—

IT IS VERY TIRESOME.

—NORTHANGER ABBEY (1817)

I CANNOT FIX ON THE HOUR,
OR THE LOOK, OR THE WORDS,
WHICH LAID THE FOUNDATION.
IT IS TOO LONG AGO.
I WAS IN THE MIDDLE BEFORE I
KNEW THAT I HAD BEGUN.

—PRIDE AND PREJUDICE (1813)

HOW WONDERFUL,
HOW VERY WONDERFUL
THE OPERATIONS OF
TIME, AND THE CHANGES
OF THE
HUMAN MIND!

—MANSFIELD PARK (1814)

DO NOT GIVE WAY TO

USELESS ALARM;

THOUGH IT IS RIGHT TO BE

PREPARED FOR THE WORST,

THERE IS NO OCCASION TO

LOOK ON IT AS CERTAIN.

—PRIDE AND PREJUDICE (1813)

PERFECTION

SHOULD NOT HAVE COME

QUITE SO SOON.

—EMMA (1815)